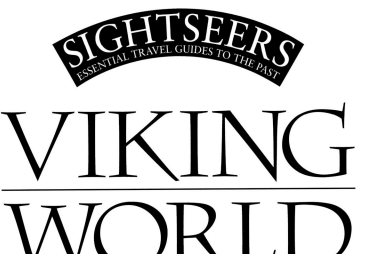

SIGHTSEERS
ESSENTIAL TRAVEL GUIDES TO THE PAST

VIKING WORLD

A GUIDE TO 11TH CENTURY SCANDINAVIA

JULIE FERRIS

KINGFISHER

NEW YORK

Written and edited by Julie Ferris and Sheila Clewley
Designer Veneta Altham

Illustrations John James
Kevin Maddison

Consultant Robin Allan

Copyright © Kingfisher Publications Plc 2000

LIBRARY OF CONGRESS CATALOGING-IN-PUBLICATION DATA
Ferris, Julie
Viking world/by Julie Ferris.
p. cm.—(Sightseers)
Includes index.
Summary: Using a travel guide format, describes
eleventh-century Viking society with information
about their home, food, clothing, customs,
voyages, and conquests.
ISBN 0-7534-5237-5
1. Vikings—Juvenile literature 2. Vikings—Civilization—
Juvenile literature. [1. Vikings.] I. Title. II. Series.

DL65 .F47 2000
9481.022—dc21

00-023998

Printed in Hong Kong/China

Contents

The Viking world 4

Traveling around 6

What to wear 8

Food and drink 10

Shopping 12

Accommodation 14

A Viking raid 16

A Viking feast 18

Leisure time 20

Temple of Uppsala 22

Exploring north 24

Eastern trade routes 26

Survival guide 28

Souvenir quiz 30

Index and acknowledgments 32

The Viking world

Situated in the northernmost reaches of Europe is one of the most exciting tourist destinations. The Viking world is a land of hardy, courageous tribes living on farms or in fortified trading communities. The climate can be harsh and the winters long, but the customs and lifestyles of these extraordinary people who have a passion for trading and raiding are fascinating. Viking lands are ripe for discovery!

Sightseers' tip
A Viking vacation is not for the squeamish. Warfare and fighting are common in their culture, and the traditional Norse religion involves both animal and human sacrifices offered to the gods.

Hedeby, a large trading town in Viking Denmark, makes an ideal base for exploration. The town is well fortified with 30-foot-high ramparts on three sides. Accommodation in town houses and nearby farms is readily available.

In 793, Lindisfarne, Scotland, was the first village raided by Vikings. They plundered the monastery, stealing treasures.

Viking explorers reach Russia in the 850s. It is a land rich in goods for which the Vikings can trade.

In 874 the first Viking settlement was established in Iceland. It is an inhospitable land, and life was hard for the pioneers.

Viking lands are widespread, so visitors must be up for a lot of traveling.

The three main Viking trading centers are Ribe, Birka, and Hedeby.

Most parts of the Viking world are ruled by wealthy and powerful kings.

The sparsely distributed Viking population is divided into three groups—Swedes, Norwegians, and Danes. They all speak the same language and have similar customs. Vikings are great seafarers—their adventuring has taken them as far as Greenland, North America, and the coast of North Africa.

Death is seen as a voyage into the unknown, so ship burials are an important funeral custom. Sometimes entire ships are buried or burned; or graves are marked by stones arranged in the shape of a boat.

In 907, the Vikings attacked the wealthy city of Constantinople. However, they failed to capture it.

Leif Eriksson explored Vinland, in North America, around 1000 and established a Viking settlement.

By 1000, Christianity had spread throughout the Viking world and become the official religion in Iceland.

5

Traveling around

The frightening carved figureheads are removed from ship prows when sailing in friendly waters so that local gods will not be upset.

Navigation is a problem on long voyages. Sailors rely on the sun and the stars to determine their position at sea. They use wooden tools to measure the height of the sun above the horizon.

If you are prone to seasickness, then the Viking world is probably not the ideal vacation destination! Inland roads are usually rough, muddy tracks, so Vikings travel everywhere they can by boat. Fortunately, their ships are the best in Europe. They are sturdy enough to cross oceans, and have flat bases for sailing along shallow rivers.

Viking boats, or longships, are sometimes referred to as "serpents of the sea" because their prows are decorated with a carving of a scary creature. Vikings believe that this monster will frighten enemy gods.

Sightseers' tip
Most Viking settlements are situated near water, and traders can be seen unloading goods onto the shore. Keep an eye out for newly arrived trading vessels if you are after souvenirs of your trip.

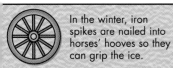
In the winter, iron spikes are nailed into horses' hooves so they can grip the ice.

Long sea voyages are undertaken only in the summer months.

! The amazing 120 ft Norwegian longship *Long Serpent* has room for 68 rowers.

To travel overland, you can walk, ride on horseback, or ask for a lift on a merchant's wagon. There are land routes between trading centers, but in the spring and summer most are muddy. Land travel is easier in the winter when the mud freezes over; skates, skis, and sleds can be used when the ground is covered in snow.

Skating is a great way to cross the Viking world's frozen lakes and rivers. Skates are made from horse, ox, or deer bone that is smoothed flat underneath. Skis are handy for traveling in the snow. It may take time to get your balance, but they are a lot of fun!

Longships can reach a speed of 17 miles per hour when sailing in a good wind. When powered by oars, the top speed is 7 miles per hour.

What to wear

Viking clothes are simple, yet practical. Men wear linen undershirts, belted woolen tunics, and pants. Women wear long, loose dresses and full-length aprons that they attach with brooches. Vegetable dyes, decorative borders, and embroidery are used to brighten the plain, but durable, clothes. The weather is usually bad, so don't forget to pack a warm wool or fur cloak.

Married Viking women cover their hair with a scarf as a sign of modesty.

The Vikings love jewelry and are famous for their beautiful gold, silver, and bronze bracelets, necklaces, and brooches.

Both men and women adorn themselves with items of jewelry, and you will be able to buy arm rings, bracelets, necklaces, brooches, and rings from local craftsmen. There should be something to fit every budget—from intricately decorated gold rings to simple bronze brooches.

Sightseers' tip

Female visitors will find the oval brooches used to fasten aprons handy. Viking women hang useful items from it, such as sewing tools, a comb, a coin purse, and keys.

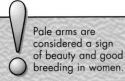 Pale arms are considered a sign of beauty and good breeding in women.

 Look for amber jewelry. Its production is an important industry in Hedeby.

 Vikings use bear, seal, and squirrel furs to make warm cloaks for the cold weather.

Cloaks are fastened using a brooch. If you are right-handed, make sure you fasten your cloak on your right shoulder so your sword arm is not restricted by the heavy material.

Most Viking women weave their own fabric and make clothes for themselves and their families. Their sewing tools are usually made from wood or bone. If you are staying in a large trading town such as Hedeby, you may be able to buy silk from Asian merchants. Silk is very fashionable, but extremely expensive.

Women wear their long hair pulled back in a bun. For men, a beard or drooping moustache is fashionable. They are kept trimmed and neat—the most fashion conscious braid their beard.

Both men and women wear slip-on leather shoes. They are usually made from goatskin or cattle hide. The most popular style is a heelless, low-cut shoe, but ankle-length or longer boots are also available for men. When the boots are worn out, they are easily replaced with new ones.

Food and drink

When it comes to food and drink, Viking families are very self-sufficient. Their farms and cattle provide them with corn and other vegetables, and meat. The rivers and seas provide a wonderful variety of fresh fish. Food is usually plentiful, particularly in the summer months, so you should eat well during your stay.

Sightseers' tip
Vikings eat twice a day—in the morning and in the evening. The meals are substantial, and you will usually be offered more than one course.

Although tables and stools are set up at mealtimes, Vikings sometimes opt to simply eat off their laps. They cut food with knives and eat with their fingers from wooden bowls and plates.

Vikings wash their food down with generous amounts of homemade beer.

Meat and fish are smoked or salted in the summer to provide food for the winter.

Vegetarians beware! Stewed or roasted meat is the main part of the Viking diet.

Why not join a hunting party and catch your own dinner? As well as hunting wild boar and reindeer on land, Vikings take to the seas to capture seals, whales, and walruses.

All cooking is done by the women of the household. They use a large metal cauldron suspended over the fire by a chain attached to the roof of the longhouse (a Viking home).

Popular dishes include meat broths and stews, barley bread, and salted fish. Homegrown vegetables and dairy products, such as milk and cheese, are also important parts of the Viking diet. All kinds of fish are eaten, including cod, herring, shellfish, and eels. Favorite dishes include seabirds, mutton, wild boar, and gull's eggs. The more adventurous visitor will have the opportunity to sample exotic fare like elk or reindeer meat.

Shopping

Although best known for their daring summer raids, the Vikings are equally impressive traders. They have established extensive trading routes all over Europe, for Viking merchants to sell their goods, such as timber, amber, and animal furs. Hedeby is a bustling trading town where you will be able to buy goods from foreign lands, as well as purchase local produce.

The town has crowded streets lined with craftsmen's houses and stalls offering a diverse selection of goods. It is the perfect place to pick up souvenirs. You can buy cloth from a weaver, a comb made of antler from a carver, a sword from a blacksmith, or silks and spices from Eastern merchants.

Traditionally, merchants used the barter system (traded goods of equal value), but payment in coins is now more common. Coins minted in Hedeby feature a Viking ship.

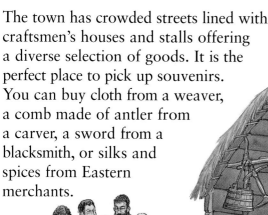

The town of Hedeby also has a flourishing slave market. People are captured on raids and sold as slaves throughout the Viking world.

Most important towns mint their own coins, usually made of silver.

 Piracy is common, so trading towns are well-defended and have lookouts.

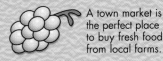 A town market is the perfect place to buy fresh food from local farms.

Blacksmiths are important craftsmen. Along with repairing tools and weapons, they make a variety of iron goods, including swords, pots, pans, and keys.

Different parts of the Viking world are famed for trading in certain goods. Timber comes from Norway, seal oil and woolen material from Greenland, and iron ore from Sweden. The Vikings also import wine from France, slaves and fur from Russia, and silk and spices from Constantinople and Persia. Goods are transported by sea, or through the country by river.

Sightseers' tip As you explore the busy market streets, you will notice that many craftsmen work outside. This is because Viking houses let in little sunlight.

Accommodation

Vikings are very hospitable, so you should have no trouble finding somewhere to stay. A farm on the outskirts of town would be perfect for a vacation house. Called longhouses, Viking homes consist of an enormous room where the entire family, guests, servants, and slaves eat, work, and sleep.

Longhouses usually don't have windows. This is because a warm house is considered more important than a well-lit one!

If you prefer to stay in the town center, you should be able to find accommodations in a town house. It will be a lot smaller than a longhouse.

The sides of a Viking longhouse are lined with earthen platforms where people sleep. There is not much furniture. Most homes have a table, a few low stools, and lockable, wooden chests to store belongings.

Women spend a lot of time in the longhouse. As well as looking after the children, they prepare and cook the food, weave cloth, and make clothes for the family.

Vikings are famed for their hospitality, often welcoming strangers into their homes.

A cozy longhouse will provide welcome shelter from the cold weather.

It is harder to find accommodation during religious festivals.

Vikings like to keep clean. Saturday is bath day, and the whole family heads for the sauna. This is usually in a small building near the longhouse. Water is thrown onto red-hot stones to produce steam.

At the center of every longhouse is a huge fireplace edged with stones. It is a vital source of heat and is used for cooking food. There is no chimney, however, so smoke escapes through a small hole in the roof.

Sightseers' tip

To maximize space in the longhouse, bedding is rolled up during the day. Important household members sleep close to the fire where it is warmest.

A Viking raid

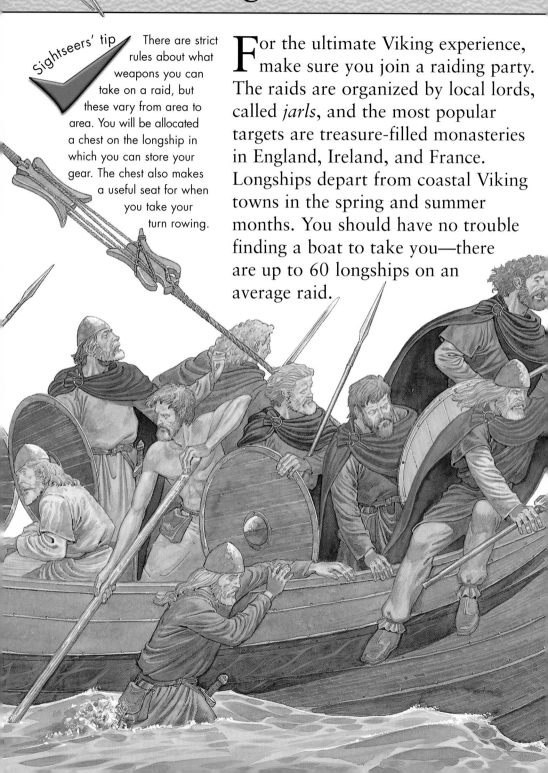

Sightseers' tip There are strict rules about what weapons you can take on a raid, but these vary from area to area. You will be allocated a chest on the longship in which you can store your gear. The chest also makes a useful seat for when you take your turn rowing.

For the ultimate Viking experience, make sure you join a raiding party. The raids are organized by local lords, called *jarls*, and the most popular targets are treasure-filled monasteries in England, Ireland, and France. Longships depart from coastal Viking towns in the spring and summer months. You should have no trouble finding a boat to take you—there are up to 60 longships on an average raid.

The most feared warriors are called *berserks*. They never wear armor.

Unguarded monasteries and towns are easy targets for Viking raids.

Fight with the sun behind you, so your opponent will be dazzled by it.

Raids are not for the fainthearted. The surprise attacks can be violent and bloody—anyone who resists the Vikings in their search for treasures to steal is killed. Viking boys are trained to fight from a young age. They practice fighting with blunt, wooden weapons, and are only allowed to use real weapons when they become adults.

Longships are also used for sea battles. After firing arrows and throwing spears at an enemy ship, the longships draw close, and hand-to-hand fighting begins.

Protective clothing is vital. If you can't afford a chain-mail shirt, get a padded leather tunic. An iron helmet and a wooden shield are useful for battles.

Axes and spears are popular weapons, but double-edged swords are higly prized. They are passed down from father to son and are given names, such as "Mail Biter."

A Viking feast

For the best in Viking entertainment, be sure to attend a feast. They are organized by local jarls and, as well as being a lot of fun, are perfect for exchanging news and gossip, and for doing business. The jarl's great hall is lined with benches, the finest tableware is brought out and the best of Viking cuisine is served. However, the most important element at any feast is the drinking—feasts can get rowdy!

Make sure you dress in your finest clothes and wear your most expensive jewelry. It is essential to look your best at a feast because the most important local Vikings will probably be there.

Servants regularly refill your drinking horn—and you have to drink it all! If you put the horn down, it falls over, so, to avoid spills, it has to be empty first.

Seating arrangements at a feast are often hierarchical—important guests have the honor of sitting next to the jarl. Occasionally, seating is decided by drawing lots.

Sightseers' tip A feast can last for several days—the longer it lasts, the more the jarl's reputation for generosity is enhanced. The best time for feasting is in the winter. Jarls who want to impress their guests host a lavish feast in midwinter, when food is scarce.

18

Women can serve food and drink, but must leave if things get too rowdy.

Feasts are held on religious holidays when sacrifices also take place.

You may have to take your turn and recite a verse—but don't worry, you can make it up!

Guests at a feast can get very boisterous, so it is common for entertainers to open with a call for silence. Poems are recited that usually include a couple of verses praising the host.

Professional poets, or *skalds*, are hired to entertain guests. Their poems are about famous battles or events in Viking history. Poems are passed from generation to generation, but have not been written down. Viking verse is famed for its descriptions of everyday things—a battle is a "game of iron," and a "speech servant" is a tongue.

Leisure time

Vikings are hard workers and do not have much free time. What spare time they do have is usually spent perfecting fighting techniques— warrior skills are extremely important to them. In fact, most Viking recreational activities involve fighting. Don't expect much relaxation on your Viking world vacation!

Sightseers' tip Vikings love to gamble. They place bets on the outcome of spectator sports such as horse fighting and wrestling.

A favorite spectator sport is horse fighting. Two stallions battle each other, egged on by their owners beating them with sticks to make them fight more viciously.

Wrestling, juggling with knives, and fencing are all dangerous sports enjoyed by Vikings. Even swimming competitions can be violent. They are not won by the swimmer with the fastest time—instead you have to try drowning the other competitors!

The Vikings do enjoy some quieter, less violent forms of entertainment. Board games are popular—the most widely played game is *hnefatafl*, a game of strategy similar to chess.

Skiing is a popular activity as well as an effective mode of transportation.

 Inventing riddles and swapping insults are considered lots of fun by the Vikings.

Look out for homemade, finely carved game pieces. They make unique souvenirs.

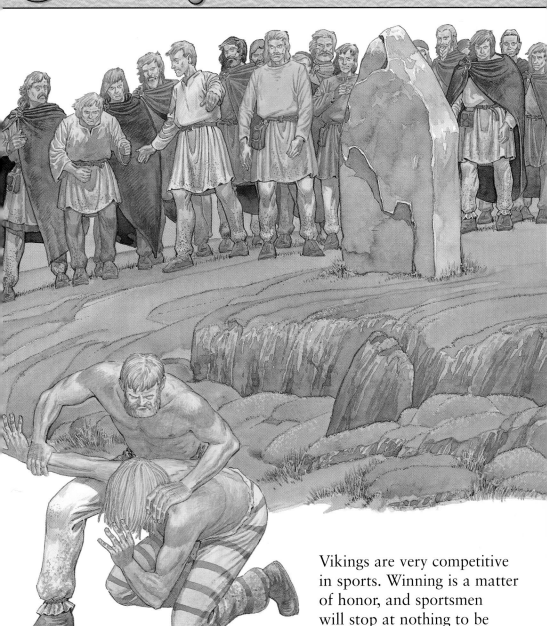

Wrestling contests take place in the open. Spectators gather around the fighters, standing close so they can get a good view of the action.

Vikings are very competitive in sports. Winning is a matter of honor, and sportsmen will stop at nothing to be victorious. In fact, it is not unusual for a wrestling contest to end in serious injury—or even death—for one of the opponents. The Vikings really do enjoy bloody spectacles!

21

Temple of Uppsala

Vikings are extremely tolerant when it comes to religion. Their own Norse religion is devoted to the worship of many gods, although the three main gods are Odin (god of war and wisdom), Thor (god of thunder), and Frey (god of nature and fertility). Increasingly, however, Vikings are converting to Christianity.

New Christian churches are being built all over the Viking world. Called stave churches, they are made of wood and have tall, triangular roofs.

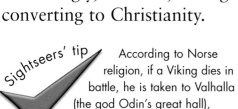

Sightseers' tip According to Norse religion, if a Viking dies in battle, he is taken to Valhalla (the god Odin's great hall), where he feasts and drinks forever.

Although Norse worship normally takes place in the open, there is a famous temple at Uppsala in Sweden that is definitely worth visiting. Huge statues of Odin, Thor, and Frey are in the temple, and every nine years a special festival is held there. A sacrifice is made of nine males of every living thing, from dogs and horses to human beings. The heads are offered to the gods, and the bodies are hung in a sacred grove.

Christian burials are increasingly popular, but you may witness a traditional chief's funeral. The chief's body is placed on a boat, which is then set on fire.

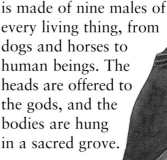

There are no priests in Norse religion. Instead, local chiefs lead the rituals and perform the sacrifices.

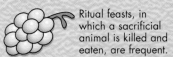 Ritual feasts, in which a sacrificial animal is killed and eaten, are frequent.

 You will see beautiful, carved statues of gods all over the Viking world.

Norse worship takes place at natural landmarks, like lakes or clusters of trees.

Many of the poems you will hear at feasts are about the Norse gods and their adventures.

23

Exploring north

If you are planning a long stay in Viking territory, why not visit one of the northern colonies? Iceland was first settled in 874 and is now a well-established community with a large population. Greenland was discovered in the 980s by Erik the Red, a Viking who was banned from Iceland for manslaughter. It is a cold, barren place, but was named Greenland to entice other Vikings to move there.

Longhouses in Iceland and Greenland are covered with peat and slightly sunk in the ground to protect against the cold.

Vikings only settled in the most habitable parts of Iceland and Greenland. They tend their crops and livestock and trade regularly with other parts of the Viking world. They export furs and hides, ropes, oil, and falcons, and import corn, iron, and timber. Timber is a necessary import because few trees grow in the extreme climate.

The only way to reach Iceland, Greenland, and Vinland is by boat.

Make sure you wear warm furs—it can be very cold in the northern colonies.

A lawspeaker is elected every three years to recite the law at the Althing.

If you are feeling adventurous, you can travel west to the newest Viking settlement. Vinland was discovered by Leif Eriksson and has a good climate and fertile land. However, its distance and the resistance of the natives put into doubt the future of this colony.

Greenland has periods of continuous sun in the summer and continuous dark in the winter. This is because it is so far north.

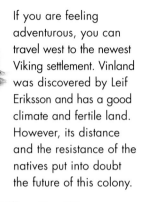

If you visit Iceland in the summer, make sure you attend the *Althing*. At this assembly laws are decided, issues are discussed, disputes are settled, and gossip is exchanged. There is also a huge fair, so it's great for buying souvenirs!

Sightseers' tip

Things are held all over the Viking world, but these mostly deal with local issues and disputes. The Althing, however, is more like a national convention.

25

Eastern trade routes

The Vikings have established extensive trade routes and settlements in the east and south through the land of the Slavs (Russia). Joining a trading expedition is a great way to see firsthand the full extent of the Viking world and its neighbors. You can visit Constantinople, the largest city in the world.

Vikings travel by boat along the huge network of rivers. When they need to change rivers, or are forced to travel overland to avoid rapids, they use logs to roll the boat over the ground.

The native Slavs call the Vikings who trade and settle in their land *Rus*, and the area is increasingly referred to as "Russia." The largest settlements are at Novgorod and Kiev.

The eastern trade routes are a must-see for serious souvenir hunters! You will be able to buy everything from furs and silk to spices and jewelry.

The Rus distrust each other so much that they will not leave the house without an armed escort.

The Rus do not cultivate their own land. Instead, food is obtained from the land of the Slavs.

Because of previous raids, Viking numbers are restricted in Constantinople.

The eastern trade routes lead to Constantinople—capital city of the Byzantine Empire (the eastern half of the old Roman Empire). The Vikings call it Miklagard, which means "the great city." It is a huge trading center, with a population of one million people.

Sightseers' tip

Constantinople is a beautiful city, famed for its fine churches and palaces. The emperor's court is known throughout the world for its elegance and wealth.

27

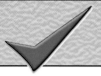

Survival guide

A visit to Viking lands is not for the fearful traveler. Life for the Vikings is tough and demanding—they work hard and play even harder. However, the adventurous and thrill-seeking globetrotter will find the customs and way of life of these northern people both challenging and fascinating.

Health

Viking life expectancy can be as high as 55 years. They are a phenomenally healthy race, although they do suffer from lice and fleas, and stomach disorders are common. Stomachaches are probably caused by traces of poisonous weeds found in the bread grain. Don't worry too much about this—if you do succumb, the discomfort will soon pass.

Warriors wounded in battle are fed onion and herb porridge. If the wound develops an onion odor, it is concluded that the intestine has been pierced by a sword and that the victim will die.

Administration

Runes are the letters of the Viking alphabet. They are made chiefly of straight lines, so carving inscriptions on wood or stone is easier. Rune stones are used to claim ownership of land, or in memory of a deceased relative.

An assembly known as the thing administers the Viking judicial system. This gathering of local landowners can last for weeks at a time. The thing discusses local problems and settles arguments about theft, murder, and land ownership.

The thing can be a social occasion as well as a judicial forum.

A duel can be fascinating to watch. But stand back!

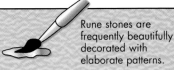
Rune stones are frequently beautifully decorated with elaborate patterns.

Law and order

Stay on the right side of the law during your visit! Strict rules and customs protect Vikings and their property—there are swift and harsh punishments for anyone caught breaking the laws. For example, a thief can expect to be hanged; and a suspected witch will die horribly by stoning, drowning, or being sunk in a swamp to suffocate.

Disagreements are often settled by a duel. Opponents face each other on a small area of land marked out by a cloth. Swords and axes are favorite weapons, and a shield is essential for defense. Duels are usually fought to the death.

? Souvenir quiz

Take your time exploring the Viking world. It is a fascinating place with plenty to see and experience. Before you leave, test your knowledge with this fun quiz. You will find the answers on page 32.

1. You will see rune stones all over the Viking world. What are runes?

a) Drawings of Vikings in battle.

b) Letters in the Viking alphabet.

c) Sign posts.

2. Why are meat and fish salted during the summer months?

a) To preserve them so that they can be eaten during the winter.

b) To improve flavor—Vikings like salty food.

c) To make them more tender.

3. What is a *berserk*?

a) A type of bear.

b) A stew made with gulls' eggs.

c) A particularly fierce warrior.

4. Why do you have to empty your drinking horn before putting it down?

a) Because it does not have a flat bottom, so the drink will spill out.

b) To show politeness—it is rude not to finish your drink.

c) So you will be served some more.

5. If you hear a Viking use the expression "speech servant," what is he talking about?

a) A slave who recites poetry and folklore.

b) A servant whose tongue has been removed to stop him gossiping.

c) The poetic term for the tongue.

6. What is a *jarl*?

a) A type of cheese extremely popular in Iceland.

b) The term used to describe a local lord.

c) A cooking pot used for making soup.

7. Frey is the Norse god of what?

a) War.

b) Wine and beer.

c) Nature and fertility.

8. What is *hnefatafl*?

a) A board game similar to chess.

b) A club carried by the god Odin.

c) A wooden storage chest.

9. Why was Erik the Red, the Viking discoverer of Greenland, banned from Iceland?

a) He was accused of stealing sheep from a neighboring farm.

b) He scrawled runic graffiti all over the local lord's longhouse.

c) He committed manslaughter.

10. Who discovered Vinland?

a) Leif Eriksson.

b) Erik the Red.

c) Vik the Viking.

11. Why do Viking women cover their hair with a scarf?

a) As a sign of modesty.

b) To keep their hair out of their eyes.

c) To keep their heads warm in the cold winter months.

Index

A
Accommodation 4, 14–15
Administration 28
Althing 25

B
Barter 12
Berserks 17, 30
Blacksmiths 13
Board games 20
Burials 5, 22

C
Christianity 5, 22
Climate 4, 8, 9, 15, 24, 25
Clothes 8–9, 14, 17, 18
Coins 12, 13
Constantinople 5, 13, 26, 27
Cooking 11, 14, 15, 18

D
Denmark 4, 5
Drink 10–11, 18, 30
Drinking horns 18, 30
Duels 29

E
England 16

Erik the Red 24, 31
Eriksson, Leif 5, 25, 31

F
Feasts 18–19, 23
Fish 10, 11, 30
Food 10–11, 14, 15, 18, 19, 30
France 13, 16
Frey 22, 31

G
Gods 6, 22, 23, 31
Greenland 5, 13, 24, 25, 31

H
Health 28
Hedeby 4, 5, 9, 12
Horse fighting 20
Houses 4, 13, 14–15
Hunting 11

I
Iceland 4, 5, 13, 24, 25, 31
Ireland 16

J
Jarls 16, 18, 31
Jewelry 8, 9, 18

L
Laws 25, 28, 29
Leisure activities 12–13, 18–19, 20–21
Longhouses 14–15, 24
Longships 6, 7, 16, 17

M
Markets 12, 13
Merchants 7, 12
Miklagard 27

N
Norway 5, 13
North America 5

O
Odin 22, 31

P
Persia 13
Poetry 19, 23, 30

R
Raids 4, 12, 16–17
Religion 4, 15, 19, 22
Runes 28, 29, 31
Rus 26, 27
Russia 4, 13, 26

S
Sacrifices 4, 19, 22, 23
Saunas 15
Ships 6, 7, 12
Shopping 8, 9, 12–13
Skalds 19
Skis 7, 21
Slaves 12, 13, 14, 26
Stave churches 22
Sweden 5, 13, 22
Swimming 20
Swords 12, 13

T
Things 25, 28, 29
Thor 22
Trading 12, 24, 26, 27
Travel 6–7, 26

U
Uppsala 22

V
Valhalla 22
Vinland 5, 25, 31

W
Weapons 16, 17, 29
Weaving 9, 12, 14
Wrestling 20, 21

....

Acknowledgments

The consultant
Robin Allan is a senior lecturer in the Scandinavian Studies department of University College London.

Additional design
Mike Davis, Jane Tassie

Picture credits
b = bottom, c = center, l = left, r = right, t = top
p.6tl The Bridgeman Art Library/University of Oslo, Norway;

p.8cl The Bridgeman Art Library/Nationalmuseet, Copenhagen, Denmark; p.12tr Werner Forman Archive/Statens Historiska Museum, Stockholm; p.17bc Werner Forman Archive/Statens Historiska Museum, Stockholm; p. 18bl Ancient Art & Architecture

Every effort has been made to trace the copyright holders of the photographs. The publishers apologize for any inconvenience caused.

....

Souvenir quiz answers

The setting for this Sightseers guide is 1010.

1 = **b)** 2 = **a)** 3 = **c)** 4 = **a)** 5 = **c)** 6 = **b)** 7 = **c)** 8 = **a)** 9 = **c)** 10 = **a)** 11 = **a)**